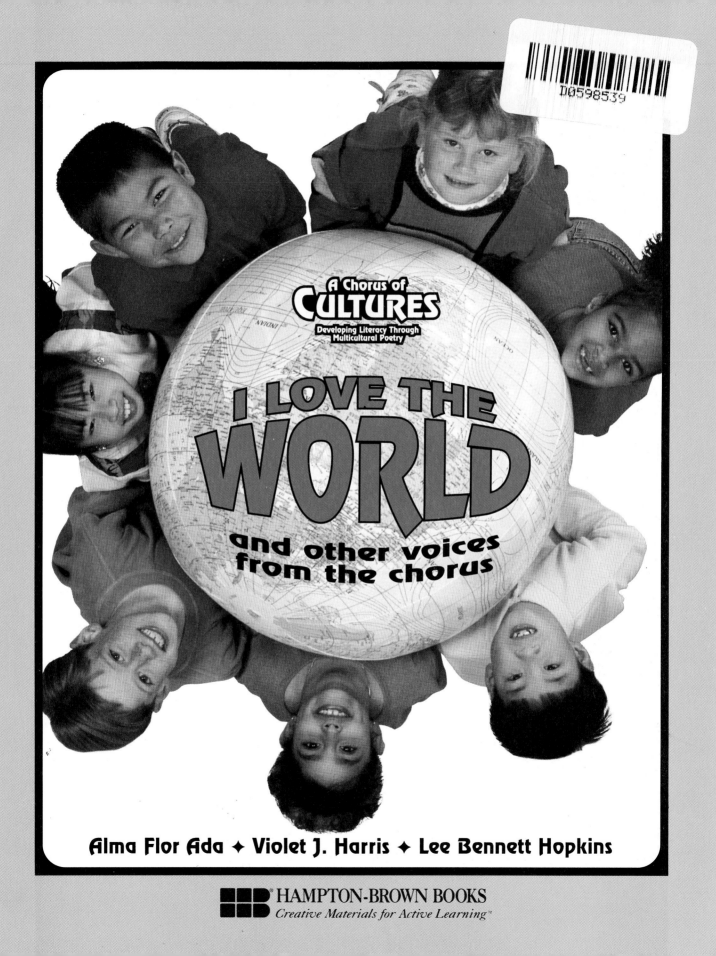

A Chorus of
CULTURES
Developing Literacy Through
Multicultural Poetry

I LOVE THE WORLD

and other voices from the chorus

Alma Flor Ada ✦ Violet J. Harris ✦ Lee Bennett Hopkins

HAMPTON-BROWN BOOKS
Creative Materials for Active Learning

Table of Contents

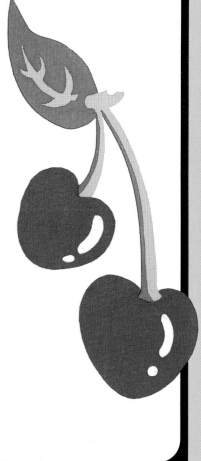

There Is a Place

on
the couch
for
grandma
and
a place on
grandma
for
me

in front
of
the
fire
and pop
ping
corn

—Arnold Adoff

Rope Rhyme

Get set, ready now, jump right in
Bounce and kick and giggle and spin
Listen to the rope when it hits the ground
Listen to that clappedy-slappedy sound
Jump right up when it tells you to
Come back down, whatever you do
Count to a hundred, count by ten
Start to count all over again
That's what jumping is all about
Get set, ready now,
             jump
                  right
                       out!

—Eloise Greenfield

Little Sister

I see her in the morning
Going down,
By the river,
In the mist.
She is brown
Like the honey,
Like the deer,
Like the ground
Of the Earth my Mother,
going round,
going round.

—*Doris Seale*

Borinquen, my little island,
Like a seashell in the sun—
On the outside, like a flower;
On the inside, there's a song.

—*Isabel Freire de Matos (original in Spanish)*
English version by Juan Quintana

THE DRUM

daddy says the world is
a drum tight and hard
and i told him
i'm gonna beat
out my own rhythm

—*Nikki Giovanni*

ORGULLO·PRIDE

Orgullosa de mi familia
orgullosa de mi lengua
orgullosa de mi cultura
orgullosa de mi raza
orgullosa de ser quien soy.

Proud of my family
proud of my language
proud of my culture
proud of my race
proud to be who I am.

—*Alma Flor Ada*

SAMPAN

Waves lap lap
Fish fins clap clap
Brown sails flap flap
Chop-sticks tap tap
Up and down the long green river
Ohe Ohe lanterns quiver
Willow branches brush the river
Ohe Ohe lanterns quiver
Waves lap lap
Fish fins clap clap
Brown sails flap flap
Chop-sticks tap tap

—*Tao Lang Pee*

HAIKU

i have looked into
    my father's eyes and seen an
    african sunset.

—Sonia Sanchez

FAMILY GIFTS

Grandpa came from Russia,
He brought a coin with him,
A coin his dad had given,
He sewed it in his hem.
He always rubbed it in his hand,
Until the picture blurred,
One day he slipped it in my palm
And didn't say a word.

—*Victor Cockburn and Judith Steinbergh*

LITTLE CORN PLANTS

Nicely, nicely, nicely, nicely,
there away in the east,
the rain clouds are caring
  for the little corn plants
as a mother takes care
of her baby.

—*Acoma traditional song*

HOME

It's a place
Just to be me
Knowing it's all right
Being me.

—Chad Bulich, age 11

Celebration

I shall dance tonight.
When the dusk comes crawling,
There will be dancing
    and feasting.
I shall dance with the others
    in circles,
        in leaps,
            in stomps.
Laughter and talk
    will weave into the night,
Among the fires
    of my people.
Games will be played
And I shall be
    a part of it.

—Alonzo Lopez

MY PEOPLE

The night is beautiful,
So the faces of my people.

The stars are beautiful,
So the eyes of my people.

Beautiful, also, is the sun.
Beautiful, also, are the souls of my people.

—Langston Hughes

GIVING

He gives double
who gives unasked.

—Arab proverb

Hands that give
also receive.

—Ecuadoran proverb

A good heart always
gives a little extra.

—Chinese proverb

A thing is bigger
for being shared.

—Gaelic proverb

El año nuevo/The New Year

Si los niños fuéramos
el año nuevo
seríamos el sol
o una estrella
para brillar con amor
y calentar
el corazón.

If children were
the new year
we'd be the sun
or a star
so we could shine with love
and warm
the heart.

—Margot Pepper's First-Grade Class

You Whose Day It Is

You whose day it is
make it beautiful.
Get out your rainbow,
make it beautiful.

—Nootka traditional song

LISTEN

every
landscape

a wondrous
story

—*Francisco X. Alarcón*

THE NEW GIRL

I can feel
we're much the same,
though I don't
know your name.

What friends
we're going to be
when I know you
and you know me!

—Charlotte Zolotow

A Lot of Kids

There are a lot of kids
Living in my apartment building
And a lot of apartment buildings
   on my street
And a lot of streets in this city
And cities in this country
And a lot of countries in the world.
So I wonder if somewhere
   there's a kid I've never met
Living in some building
   on some street
In some city and country
   I'll never know—
And I wonder if that kid and I
   might be best friends
If we ever met.

—Jeff Moss

If They Hate Me

If they hate me
    they
are
    sick
and
    hurt
and
    need
    some
    kind
of
    help.

I will
    stay
right
    here.

—*Arnold Adoff*

The Day You Were Born

The beautiful things
  that are in this world
were born the same day
  as you;
the sun was born,
  the moon was born
and the stars
  were born then, too.

—Mexican traditional song
English version by Suzanne Crain

The BEAUTIFUL

Above, above,
The birds flying.
Below, below,
The flowers on the earth.

In the mountains, the mountains,
The trees growing.
In the ocean, the ocean,
The fish of the sea.

Here ends my song,
The beautiful world.

—Hawaiian traditional song

I LOVE THE World

I love you, Big World.
I wish I could call you
And tell you a secret:
That I love you, World.

—*Paul Wollner, age 7*

BEING JEWISH

feels like having
the whole team
on your side
whether you
strike out
or not

—Josh Weinstein

Dirt Road

A shiny stone by a dirt road
So small, yet so beautiful
I picked it up. So beautiful it was
    I put it down
        And walked on.

—Calvin O'John

Mama

Mama was funny
was full of jokes
was pretty
dark brown-skinned
laughter
was hard hugs
and kisses
a mad mama
sometimes
but always
always
was love

—*Eloise Greenfield*

Matriarch

my dark
grandmother

would brush
her long hair

seated out
on her patio

even ferns
would bow

to her splendor
and her power

—Francisco X. Alarcón

My Beloved Country

Native country
  like a branch of starfruit.
Let the sun climb up
  to pick it every day.
Native country
  small like a bamboo bridge.
Native country
  like a child that understands.
Let the child grow up
  to be a gentle person.

—*Trung Nguyen, 9th grade*

Two Little Sisters

Two little sisters went walking one day,
Partly for exercise, partly for play.
They took with them kites
    which they wanted to fly,
One a big centipede, one a great butterfly.
Then up in a moment
    the kites floated high,
Like dragons that seemed
    to be touching the sky!

—Chinese traditional rhyme

My Father

My father doesn't live with us.
It doesn't help to make a fuss;
But still I feel unhappy, plus
   I miss him.

My father doesn't live with me.
He's got another family;
He moved away when I was three.
   I miss him.

I'm always happy on the day
He visits and we talk and play;
But after he has gone away
   I miss him.

—*Mary Ann Hoberman*

Summer Song

Summer, summer and a shell,
white sand and parasol,
cold red watermelon,
one orange peach.
Coffee house, vanilla sundae,
cherry peeking from the drips,
whipped cream mountain,
  all these almonds,
apricots and grapes.

Summer, summer and a shell,
white sand and parasol,
cold red watermelon,
and a deep blue sea.

—Ilana Israeli (original in Hebrew)
English version by Mazal Jaret and Judith Steinbergh

Mirror Mirror

People keep asking where I come from
says my son.
Trouble is I'm american on the inside
      and oriental on the outside.

No Kai
Turn that outside in
THIS is what American looks like.

—*Mitsuye Yamada*

The Palet Man

"Soursop, coconut, mango, lime!"
Neville, Arjune, Jasmine and I
run down the street
to the palet man.
Count out our change
as we get in line.
Wait our turn
and *then* decide:
soursop, coconut, mango, or lime?

—*Lynn Joseph*

My Sister's Just Like Me

My sister and I are almost the same
when she gets angry
she wants to throw something
just like me
she loves my dad
she's always there when my dad needs her
just like me
she likes to wear jeans and shirts
just like me
she likes to read Vietnamese
just like me
she likes computers
just like me
but when she writes
it's about her private life
she has secrets
just like me

—*Phuc Huynh, 5th grade*

MY TRIBE IS CHOCTAW

My tribe is Choctaw
    and the name reminds
    me of chocolate!
I don't have an Indian
    name but I wish I did.
One that means the
    glorious sunrise and
    the heavenly sunset.
One that means the
    dazzling wild flowers
    with their sensuous
    scent of perfume.
One with extraordinary
    waterfalls crashing
    over rocks sending
    colorful rainbows into
    the blue peaceful sky.
One that means the
    beautiful gifts
    of earth.

—*Victoria Wilson, 6th grade*

Grandma and the Thunder

I hear Ah-Pau in the kitchen
cooking thunder in her wok.
I hear it rolling and clattering over the fire
like some live animal. Ah-Pau
pushes the hair from her eyes,
stands away as it hisses
garlic and scallion,
   bok-toy and "black cloud,"
breathing black mushroom, choong-toy
"snow cloud" and snowpea,
   snorting and rocking
like some heavenly dragon. Gently
she soothes it to a simmer, talking
to it softly, asking it to behave.
Steam rises beneath her spatula.
Storm-scent clings to her hair.

—Sarah Chan